CAMPFIRE RADIO RHAPSODY

CAMPFIRE RADIO RHAPSODY

ROBERT EARL STEWART

Mansfield Press

Printed in Canada

Library and Archives Canada Cataloguing in Publication

Stewart, Robert Earl, 1974-
Campfire radio rhapsody / Robert Earl Stewart.

Poems.
ISBN 978-1-894469-53-1

I. Title.

PS8637.T4955C35 2011 C811'.6 C2011-902755-0

Editor for the Press: Stuart Ross
Design: Denis De Klerck
Typesetting: Stuart Ross
Cover Photo: iStockphoto
Author Photo: Cristina Naccarato

The publication of *Campfire Radio Rhapsody* has been generously supported by the Canada Council for the Arts and the Ontario Arts Council.

Canada Council for the Arts
Conseil des Arts du Canada

Mansfield Press Inc.
25 Mansfield Avenue, Toronto, Ontario, Canada M6J 2A9
Publisher: Denis De Klerck
www.mansfieldpress.net

for Jennifer,
and for Nathanael, Jonah, and Thomasin

CONTENTS

11 I'm Bleeding
12 Transmission
13 Caution: Pigeons
14 We Press to Each Other Through the Glass of Days
17 A Moon Called the Moon
18 Broadcast
19 Rosary Trail
20 Message from the Night Desk
21 The County Reporter
30 Anecdotal Evidence in Floodplain and Erosion Control
31 The Narrows
32 Barn Burning
33 Fortunate Son
34 Who Has Seen the Muslin Bear?
36 Bangkok Winter
37 New Orchid Society
38 Nights in the Old Testament
39 Siamese Masquerade
42 Löwendenkmal
43 The Beautiful Lake
44 Surrogate for Here
45 Robot
48 Veins
49 We Live Near Al Capone
50 Not Yet, Thomasin
51 Fire Escape
52 Forrester
53 Christmases
54 So Long, Vince Guaraldi
55 Disappearer
57 The Day I Didn't Go Skydiving

59 Thurston Owl
60 The Rise of the Tortoise Lobby
62 Dweller on the Threshold
63 Small Shelter
64 Self-Diagnosis with Bullwhip
65 Nothing by Mouth After Midnight
67 Cyprus Lake
68 White Lies (About Hackberry Emperors)
70 Deus Ex Machina
71 Shadows of Individual Trains
72 Rivermouth
73 Fully Engulfed
74 They Will Take My Island
75 Titus Livius
78 The Forever of Old Ice
79 From a Hotel Alexandra
80 Metal Gods in the Foothills
82 The Band of the Ceremonial Guard
84 Great Western Amusements
85 Malt Shaft
86 He Disavows His Original Coyote Population Estimate
88 Debris Field Investigation
90 Also Known as the Yo-Yo Man
92 A Wind-Aided Fire
95 Frozen Like Floating

The terrible channels where
the wind drives me against the brown lips
of the reeds are not all behind me. Yet
I trust the sanity of my vessel; and
if it sinks, it may well be in answer
to the reasoning of the eternal voices,
the waves which have kept me from reaching you.

—Frank O'Hara
"To the Harbormaster"

I'M BLEEDING

The longer I looked through the trees, the more I saw.
And I saw everything—and it wasn't just trees, but the wind,
the rushes, white berries on red filaments in purple leaves;
deer runs through a whispering sea of reeds
that moved in waves to the river's edge.
And if I left the boardwalk
and lit out into the catacombs beneath the cloud deck
of amber and brown and crimson, would I stumble
on a mother and her fawn curled in a cove and be kicked
by the buck's black blades,
falling into the matted basket of their warmth,
as they arc off through the rushes?

TRANSMISSION

Stumbling upon the wreckage of a piano in the woods
you immediately regret having ditched your lessons
to hide in the mansions of New Zebedee, Michigan.

It dawns on you that these are the last few minutes of that dream
where the steering wheel is gone
and control is a bolt that hurts your fingers.

Boot prints follow you through the snow,
staggered like the buttery leaves that clutch a few branches,
like sturgeon against the woods—

all the way back to the right-of-way where people cut
down Christmas trees during breaks in the traffic.
You sit down to hunt and peck

through the original score. You're wearing a tuxedo.
You assume that whoever is laughing
is doing so to avoid some unflattering self-awareness.

And then the separation: an ice shelf that will inevitably
be compared to Manhattan.
Then crows in the red velvet cake of the shoulder

after the scraping of antlers and the clatter of hooves,
and the growing knowledge

that every bridge must be shorter in the winter.

CAUTION: PIGEONS

In the seasons after the last carrier pigeons
expired in the folds of a Samaritan's shirt on the side of a highway
near a jackknifed trailer

we walked the damp streets near the science centre
after the radio club meeting; empty rookeries and antennas
on the embassy rooftops.

We became Saturday-morning spooks
through the city—
your taste for thin ties and raincoats
in the wharf district; homemade lake dirigibles sneaking
up the river and entering the harbour—

drawn to the glowing receiver
in the space above the garage; obscured
by phonetic hotel alphabets and the echoes
of uniform November. The campfire radio encryption.
The sound of the trucks down Locust Avenue.
The uncanny box scores.

We wanted only that *The Swedish Rhapsody*
play again over the sweaty sheets
as feathers fell black against the moon.

WE PRESS TO EACH OTHER THROUGH THE GLASS OF DAYS

I think back to those early experiments with the windsurfer,
    how you averted your eyes—

my hubris a horrible blight on your sense of station.
    Even when I tried to see it as your demurring, I failed
        and dove into pockets of sun and silt.

Nothing was ever right.
    I'm not sure how we made it. I'm not sure
        how we didn't couple out of spite

in the guest cottage. Your father let you drive the road
    to the store—his car had the taxi cab action back seat.
        It swallowed me up, a forgotten snack

smelling like forest loam, and sun and lake;
    my face clearing up from the sun, drying
        and browning as I read Zindel, Korman, and Pinkwater

in the wind until dinner, when the satellite barbecue hit,
    a smoking wreckage with sausage on the lake stone patio.
        Later there would be five or six bears

at the dump, delighted to find your early pads,
    and you would cry.
        The timing could not have been worse—

or better—and I found the box decorated like a meadow
    in the guest cottage bathroom, and
        tried one on with my bathing suit,

just to experience *that* between my legs—
  and felt strangely more
    masculine in those moments swimming around

in the lake than at any time previous—
  and that's when I found the axe in the shallows
    with the rocks and the bluegills. It was rusted

and mossed over and I asked my father to refurbish it
  for me; and we cut wet wood with it in the rain
    and found a toad in a rotted limb

we cleaved in two. I was worried it would usurp me
  for your fascination, but your watching told me I was wrong
    as I wrapped my fist around it

and brought it, blinking and flexing its tympanum,
  up from the mould and wood, and showed you it was alive;
    that I was not like the brothers from St. Catharines

who would skip them across the water, screaming
  the counts in vicious celebrations
    that reverberated like names around the lake.

When I found those injured "stones"
  paddling helplessly in the boathouse,
    where they'd limped in a long useless arc,

I cried and asked my father how to fix it,
  but the pike came in at night and finished the job.
    I had the axe; I had your eye.

I had my books and one more week.
    And there was a lot of pop to be drunk between now and then,
        and a tough portage that would require you

to take off your shoes
        in the marsh.

A MOON CALLED THE MOON

The tide raises all boats.
All boats rise with the tide.
Rising, boats; a moon.

The tide raises all
boats and answers to the moon.
Boats. The moon. Some light.

The tide raises all
boats. Boats, the moon, and some light.
Rising: boats; a moon.

BROADCAST

A radio through the trees.
A bike or a harmonica through the trees.
Voices and light through smoke through the trees.
Through the trees, the depression of a French
press and the fall of a Jenga tower.
Leather off skin; leather on air; leather
on leather. A mocking cry of:
Eddie, where's your bird?
Somewhere, amidst the casual nudity
of changed shirts and bathing suits
stepped-out-of, someone
is being bent over in a tent,
and entered like a tent—
flaps pulled back
and a puddle at the entrance
where the shoes are piled.
I don't need to see it to know it.
And in the closeness of the tent
I can smell it, and under cover
of darkness I can hear it—
badger breathing,
and cries
muffled into handfuls of sandy clothes
slipping through the night trees
like foreign voices I understand.
Like campfire transistor radio.

ROSARY TRAIL

Someone just yelled someone else's name across the lake.
It was not mocking or joyous, and it could have been Charles,
Carla or Joe,

                                        and it was filled with concern, even fear.
Wildcats or raccoons were brawling on the Rosary Trail
at the feet of the gothic virgins from the Diocese of London.

I put down the book I was reading, got up from my chair,
and locked the door. Then I got some more chips
from the cottage kitchen and returned to my chair,

where I rocked, expectantly,
waiting to hear the name again.

MESSAGE FROM THE NIGHT DESK

They will be burning down the prairie today,
starting at 9. Please cover this.
Invaders will perish in the glacial furnace;
native species will flourish in the fired earth.
There will be a helicopter looking
like it's about to crash over the flames
all afternoon. Other things to look out for:
They will be reenacting the cover
of *The Certainty Dream*. Please make mention
of the bottle of rye that refuses
to melt, and the deer that refuse to run,
out of fear and loss; the fried snakes, and
the stash of girlie mags in the old stump.
This will run on page one if you get a good shot.

THE COUNTY REPORTER

I. GULLY PARTY

Crows fight over a piece of meat in a field
near a stretch of tracks in a heat too early.
Bone shards and gristle, ground to tallow
and enlarged like suet coins beneath the wheels,
tumble in the loosestrife and elderberry
down the embankment. Pulverized along the tracks
by a town's length of steel and grain in a night as blue
and perfect as the sun's iron-black core,
a boy, whose parents, on a couch somewhere
over the fields, still expect their son to slouch
through the door triumphant from a night in the Gully.
But the engineer picked him up in the candlepower
of the lamp as he climbed
from the kudzu-choked swamp beneath the trestle—
a trestle he did not stumble along in a frantic
attempt to outrun the freight of his days
in the darkness, crossing into the fields
with the doomsday whistle and the scream
of the brakes at his back for long enough
for the moon to change positions. And in the dry dust
of morning, I'm walking over parabolas of tread
towards this turbulence, blue and green like flies,
where wrapped in denim, stretched and twisted
like taffy in the purple beaks of the crows whose wings
kick up dust where I've walked,
some teenager the body-removal people missed
in a night-fallow field outside of Puce.
The flesh is brutish red and going bad in the heat.

2. WAVE POOL

Your daughter, just so you know, was too sad
to cry when she got to the scene,
the body-removal people having already heaved you
into a bag, headed to their rambling mansion in the corn
where they will break you out of position
and make you look like a distant cousin.
She removed some paperback novels
and a tartan blanket dripping with kernels of windshield
from the back seat, before disappearing
into the crowd. I only tell you this
because certain connections formed as I stood, helpless
in my objectivity, looking at you slumped
and unrecognizable before the sirens,
before the interminable procedure
of the accident scene: the protocols of recreation
and death; and the unspoken non-protocols of
dirt and blood—
before a constable escorted you across
the threshold of my understanding
by leaving your damp, brown wallet
open faux-absently on his clipboard, whispering,
"I probably shouldn't say anything."
And with that you transformed from a dead blackjack dealer,
broken beyond beauty against the steering column,
to the mayor of the days of the scar across my chin—
a scar earned trying to impress K-W girls
with a handstand in the shallows of a wave pool,
but crumpling and bleeding out on the gradual beach.
The mayor of the days of hope—
in the bosom of Auto Pact, in the shadow
of Detroit—that we would have an hydraulic amusement
to call our own, pounding away endlessly

all summer on the riverfront. But what we got
was a laughing stock, and nothing.
Even in death, detractors
and allies line up in my phone queue
to say you never found your way to shore,
that it was the wave-pool idea
that brought you to your knees, wearing
a dealer's vest, fingers numb from twenty-one,
palms shot through with hearts and diamonds,
your eyes wearing coins of clubs and spades,
a bow-tie when you passed through sleep, phasing
into the oncoming lane, as if to drive to work in reverse.
And now, with your Buick glacially still
in the stifling corridors of corn, struck down
just north of the Dairy Freez, just south
of the last place you drew breath,
I snap the shot that will become synonymous
with your death: the dull grey hood rippled
in curtains of impact, as clear a sign of defeat
as a ragged, vulnerable scar,
like the story I have to write tonight,
about the jokes that cut like a city-wide
conspiracy of daggers, where "wave pool"
becomes synonymous with failure,
a byword for futility in a city that fails mightily
every time it tries something new.
I wanted to slink off
into the endless undulations of corn and cry—
the memory of your long delayed, final
synaptic flare running through your body
like a mechanical wave,
like the worm across my chin.

3. HEAD, HEART, HANDS, HEALTH

I wish I knew a young man who walked through town
with a cow on a rope. You'd see them, together,
eating lunch, watching little league games—
you'd hear its bell ring in the morning
when it went down to bring in the paper.
But I don't know that boy, or that cow, now.
But I did. In the bleating of the 4-H barn,
the loud meaningless prayer of livestock
incessant in a distraction of blue ribbons
at the Harrow Fair. One pinned to
the marbled shoulder of a brown calf
lying in the hay against the barn wall.
Her boy on her golden flank,
crying his heart out for her,
under a single, naked bulb
hanging from a wire of frayed fabric.
Betrayed by my city-softness, I cried
with the boy, unable to trip the shutter,
there in the aftermath of the auction,
preserving the fruit of sadness
in the jar of memory's inaction, realizing:
Maybe I'm not who I want to be,
who I want people to think I am, behind this camera.
Not hard. Not unflappable.
But finding a line I'm not willing to cross
in animal grief, the ache of lost pets.
But I won't spare the two farmers who stand
under cheese-grater seed caps,
their eagerness like gravy on their chins,
swelling out of their Arrow shirts,
protectors of rural pragmatism
and masculinity—paragons of

head, heart, hands, and health—
vultures hiding behind their drugstore aviators
talking out the sides of their mouths,
waiting out the boy's despair—
his childish fondness for an animal he's raised
from embryo; his weakness for kind eyes
that reflect back a barn of the doomed—
where, after nine months of fattening and
whispering in a whiskery ear,
it dawns on him what he has done.
As tears roll, bronze breakers in a pasture,
I capture the farmer's sarcoma noses,
their cruel, wet, meat-speculating mouths—
an archive of their simple darkness;
two weathered stereotypes,
as mean and straight as barn boards;
as internally twisted as the cutting-room rushes
considered too boring by metro desk,
left on the light table, some small posterity
for their concupiscence. How happily
I would have tucked bills into their breast pockets,
dispatching them to the pie auction,
just to live with myself a bit longer—
to see the boy and his cow grow old together,
shop for organic vegetables together,
the picture of the men who tried to vivisect them
growing yellow on the fridge. In the sunglasses of one,
dark eyes that will keep you up at night are ghosts
behind the smoky lenses,
while the other's hands hang frozen,
throttling the life out of some familiar trauma
you cannot understand or change.

4. POST-ABATTOIR BLUES

A knife clenched in his teeth—
a hunting knife, with serrated bone-cutting edge,
a tooled grip, and a compass mounted in a bauble
on the end, in case he gets lost in the hooves
and intestines, bones and organs
heading towards the screw.
His polyester work pants' twin creases
slice through the sweetbread surface, and he is waist-deep
in heart and mind. He is alive in the make-up
your wife will wear, the fragrances you will taste—
a folk hero in the rendering plant,
where some have lost their sense of smell
through a subconscious act of the will.
But mid-flight, he can smell
the lily-white coveralls of the assessors;
he can smell their pens checking off the infraction—
the slaughter needed to be over
before the payloads of offal were poured
like a meal into the pit, the death of an animal
in the plant a sacrilege in a place
requiring ultra-sonic destruction of flies
lest the air become exoskeleton
around the miasma of churning aspic.
The boss is pressed like a ham against
his glassed-in aerie overlooking the pit,
watching the piglet struggle,
bleating for its shredded kin
in a sargasso of heifer, ewe, prize pony,
and Rhode Island Red—
somehow this wriggling piglet alive
in this batch, destined for the cosmetic houses
of Paris. But today, the hero

intercepts the foreman's hand
reaching for the kill switch,
and there will be no stopping of the screw:
backing it off, emptying the pit, disinfecting, testing,
incinerating the cosmetic suet on the other side
of the insatiable blind worm.
The pig screams for mercy, as the screw draws near,
busting gristle, popping skulls,
using a brisket against flesh in an orgy
of grinding and juice. And it does not see
the man approaching from the south, knife clenched in his teeth,
camouflaged, until the last second, when,
for a moment, the piglet looks like a happy child
and swims towards him, smiling in a gorgeous oblivion.

5. VISITING THE PIE MUSEUM

I checked out the pie museum today.
One of them was bleeding lemon in beads,
light from the palms of the suffering saviour,
in the glass-walled reliquary
by the takeout window. A woman was
passed out at the lunch counter, face down
in the Lifestyles section. I daresay
I was the only person reading
Chinese Whispers in there today over
my peameal and deep-fried dill pickle.
A jaunty old guy with amulets
flirted with the maiden-aunt waitresses
who bore coffee carafes like pitchers
of scented water to a patriarch.
He told them he was waiting for his daughter
and son-in-law. He tells them this every day.
I am the only person surprised when
the woman raises her head from the newsprint
and goes back to work behind the counter.

6. I HEART TORNADOES

I spent the morning with a funnel cloud,
its grey glide over the low Kingsville soy
like a glacier, so low I could hear its mechanism,
following it out to Colchester Beach—
travelling together
like old companions, my arm out the window
to touch its wisp across the aisle
of plausibility and concession road—
where I sat at the top of tall steps down the bluff
while lightning licked the lake.

ANECDOTAL EVIDENCE IN FLOOD PLAIN AND EROSION CONTROL

And one day, the river simply rose up—
a mirror that stood at the bridge,
hazy with hockey games, with all the river
piling up behind it, all one thing like a mountain.

And perilous cold and dark, the part that was still running
spread out behind the ice dam
and went right through living rooms
like a bright black knife edge.

And at an unseasonably warm moment,
all the docks north of the bridge floated
in the air and collapsed into the channel
that ran between corrugated fires.

And the dam fell back on itself and the bridge
gave a slow, breech birth to a fist of glass
that scoured the bed to shield stone, pulverizing
pleasure craft in dry dock and sun room.

And they gathered on the public wharf
and saw their possessions, including a lit
grill complete with salmon, floating in open water.
And, swan-like, the paper trick of the town unfolded.

THE NARROWS

There's always something burning in Detroit.
Palls rise like trees throwing their carbon sinks
up in exasperated defeat, to hang there
as inverted vascular systems; to be blown
over the core, where a herd of deer
grows like a hornets' nest on the console
of an old TV—the screen kicked in but showing
the inferno blazing around it;
the cathode tube doing whatever it does in the dark,
for free, for everyone.

They built a fort here because it's the narrowest point
along the Great Lakes. They could fire across
at the Mission and monitor
the progress of the King's Navy at dock
at the lakehead. And when the king came
on a secret visit, they could see him
through a spyglass
and they commented on the cut
of his raiment, and on his wig.

But they did not consider the return fire—
parabolas no less equally beautiful across the river
and pounding the timbers of the Pontchartrain.
Pounding the Midwestern flatness before it was anything
but the west. And when Cadillac
was out of town, a priest and a sergeant were killed
outside the walls. Deserters cannibalized
one of their own, and great plumes went up then, too.

BARN BURNING

Abraham Lincoln's death chair is anonymous
amidst America's foremost collection of baubles and gewgaws
and the lacquered black boat of the Kennedy assassination limousine,
which sits behind red velvet ropes, flirting with the pococurante:
polished, debonair, and obsidian sterile.

Whereas Lincoln's brains and blood soak
the purple upholstery like hair oil, and run in the maple scrollwork
like stain.

Why doesn't the museum ring out with the hush
of those who lined the embankments and trestles as the funeral train
worked its way back to Illinois? Do any companies perform
Tom Taylor's farce and fall to pieces halfway through Act III, Scene 2,
then into silence forever?

When will they come to claim their ark
and carry it away before them, its voice the shape of sitting,
blazing like a tobacco barn in the night, calling out
through the spark-lit darkness to the soldiers
who pursued an actor south across the Potomac?

FORTUNATE SON

The memorial silhouette of Pvt. Michael J. Mulherin
has been defaced again. His brain was cooked by radars
while he tanned on the high decks of a destroyer
in the Sea of Japan. Somewhere, his fellow Detroiters
were getting chewed up and spit out of the jungle.
The marble is scrawled with cocks, swastikas, a pile of shit
at his boot heels, a gang tag for a face. He made it home
and died in a terrible hospital. Grown men are being taught
to bag groceries in the outreach clinic at VVA #9,
Woodward Avenue, some twenty years after the last chopper
left Saigon. In the clubhouse, a man in a long beard and trench coat
reads poetry that should be etched into the back window
of a pickup. They play "Switching to Glide,"
which apparently has something to do with their war.
A Pomeranian named Sweet Apple sits in the nest
of red vinyl and foam of a broken-down bar stool.
Her owner takes out her teeth when the music gets slow.
From the steel briefcase where he keeps his poetry comes a photo
of a man's severed head, hanging from a shred of flesh
on a barbed-wire fence. *I did that,* he says. *I did that on my watch
with my bayonet.* They send me back across the border in a cab
on their dime, blind drunk.

WHO HAS SEEN THE MUSLIN BEAR?

Every play I've seen lately features
significant incidents on bridges.

In one, a young girl's mouth is opened
over the lower rung of the railing. Her teeth
and tissue rain down into the river below.

In the other, an energy executive
is gunned down by commandos, his blood
and guts raining down into the river below.

In one, the river is light; in the other,
the river is sound. In both, there is a pair
of baby shoes, and in one

a prop is removed from the set
during rehearsal—

an event that will significantly alter
everything that is to come. A cast meeting
is called. Better this is confronted

in rehearsal than during the festival. The prop,
a doll, was not on the bureau
when it should have been

and cues and blocking
fell all to shit. The person responsible

for removing the prop—
little more than a twist of cloth
in the shape of some horrific bear—

apologizes for the lack of consideration,
and we all consider the ramifications

to the story; we are all forced along channels
that spread out like tributaries
full of sediment's remorseful baggage

through a river delta,
like so many guns over mantelpieces.

BANGKOK WINTER

O, bathmat!
You make the upstairs smell like cheese,
you killed Thomas Merton,
and you make the skin of my toes peel off
in sheets,

white and whorled like your innocuous
field of worms, smouldering;
a flat, wet fire
in a Bangkok winter.

NEW ORCHID SOCIETY

The novelty of seeing people
you know in a window has worn off.
The orchid society is corrupt,
their leader the type of man

you suspect likes to be tied up
and beaten. Ex-photographers
are being crucified
on the roof of the brickyard,

and one of them is in one of those bands who jealously
          guard their sound. They're laying bed tracks
in the studio tonight. There's an electric piano
                    in the Persian rug alcove.

And the singer:
          her hair is dead and wild
                    like an old man's backyard.

NIGHTS IN THE OLD TESTAMENT

When the children act out scenes from the Bible,
Jonah is always the lamb
laid out for sacrifice on the unlit pyre of the living room floor—
the dove beneath the lightsabre raised

above his sister's head,
inculcated in his brother's chanting of the national anthem,
all ribs, belly button, and the future's dimple.
But martyrdom is not really his style. The role he covets
is that of the messenger

carried in the pink cathedral arches
of the leviathan, where the initials of the rebellious sons
who lit out for Spain before him

show up like shadow-rimmed scars
in the guttering blue fire of ship boards.

Beached and breaking past
the lolling tongue, he's the dove from the ark
of the baleen system, striding forth
with a staff and spangled in sea vines,

soaked in the miraculous facets
of the evening that allow him to be the dove
and the lamb between dinner and bed,

in the descending shadow of the blade cutting
across the Persia of the rug.

Never mind there are no whales in this sea.
Just the swaying constellation of the whale shark.

SIAMESE MASQUERADE

That was the summer strays could be seen
sunning in packs on the steep slopes of roofs. We heard them jumping
from house to house, landing above our bed in the morning,
then into the stately trees where they hung like leopards
over the branches to cool, languid and sovereign in the day,
coming down to the ground, stalking the garden voles
in the star field of trilliums at dusk, then moving
like tactical units down the alleys, their fur flashing
in the velveteen drone.
It was no place to be embarrassed by indolence
or defecation.

The weather turned and a huntless torpor began.
We chased flashing foil pie tins around the backyard
and refilled them with food, and when the devil horns of hostas
marked the spring, the pie tins persisted, as did the huntless torpor.
A generation was minted under the decks,
curled nursing like purring slugs in the raspberries,
oblivious to the playful interrogations
of the field;

neophytes before the fetid, wet gutting; the retracting of the tools
from the quarry. And the tube worlds of rats began to unwind
under those same birthing porches, conjured
like rapacious worms out of the habits of misguided husbandry.
And a tolerance spread, a thinned blood that thickened
into another winter.

I looked out my back door into the eyes of cats powerless
over our generosity. They begged me with their matted winter faces
to help them quit us. Rats moved unmolested amongst them

in the cascade of dry food I threw down the back steps.
They asked it as plain as speaking.

A seamstress from the lite opera company helps me sew something up
in grey flannel: like footed pajamas with an eared hood and
an elegant Siamese mask—
that first night with the suit, I step out into the yard and meet them
beneath the star magnolia's nakedness.

My vision blurs in the pulsing black pool of their thrumming
under the citrus moon, in the grapefruit of their urine;
fecal mud mixed with the spark smell of cold.
I luxuriate in their funk. It covers me in my cat suit.
And then we're running

in a big, joyous pack along the fences—
I lead them in this, the silent parkour of tail balance and fang,
and I'm a 300-pound puma and I pounce
on a rat and its intestines bloom
from the fur cavity like a pink carnation
in the snow rut. My crew moves in, sniffing the steaming bowel
flower, and then shares the slickness.

Night after night into the spring, we run our line. I'm crushing
moles, field mice, and rabbits in my hands,
shaking the meat and offal right from the pelt.
They teem at my feet and begin to fight—
more for the blood than my approval,

and of this I approve even more. And when I collapse in bed,
leaner and deft and reeking of the hunt, I am unburdened
before our creator as they grow shinier, deadlier,

more cunning, insidious, and so impressed with themselves that
I would turn away in modesty from their lovemaking
in the spring—when they return to the roofs, virile,
and staggering under the weight of so much conquest.

I wash the suit and hang it out to dry one day,
and forget it there on the line. Wakened in the night
by a horrible lowing, I look from the back door to see them
gathered beneath my empty form where it twists a bit in a zephyr,
thinking maybe I have been called home.

LÖWENDENKMAL

I was conceived in Switzerland. It was the fall of '73,
in a hotel at the foot of the Matterhorn. In the lobby
you could buy wooden music-box replicas.
The paddle wheel turned as "Edelweiss" played.
There are pictures of them hitchhiking. My father
has sideburns and Ray-Bans. My mother
in her slip in the gloaming room. She looks
over her shoulder as she eats something
at a small desk. They went there thinking
they would never have me. A lion dying
in the saddest and most moving piece of rock
in the world. A Belgian trucker who sent Christmas cards
until one year they stopped. At home, the grass grew
imperfectly. Appointment reminders whispered by the phone.
These people by the lake, and at the airport in Zurich,
are younger than I am now. The camera these were shot with
sits in a cabinet next to a canister in a velvet bag.
I spent hours with this album. It was like a memory—
like I was in those mountains with them, looking out
from the hotel of her stomach. When I see Zermatt,
it looks like home. When I see Lucerne,
it makes me cry.

THE BEAUTIFUL LAKE

He's seven and he's standing in front of
Adolphe Vogt's *Coming Storm During Harvesting.*
He's an amber-gold field against the purple storm—
a stand of birches turning the rare white
of their backsides to the crescendo, the lightning of the whip—

and he says he will paint a painting called *The Beautiful Lake,*
and it will be of people gathered in a church,
looking at a piece of paper and praying.

I am afraid for him. Buoyed and afraid
as he sits on a bench before
a cartoonish painting of a doe-eyed blonde's head
wreathed in blossoms,

and says, "There was a huge fire at her town
and she was the only one to survive it," when told
what the painting's called: there are bunnies in space,
kittens in baskets; bizarre hats, and deer sleeping in trees.

When we see where the band is setting up for a wedding,
we consider running home and putting on
our nice shirts and ties and coming back for dinner,
claiming to be cousins of the bride.

SURROGATE FOR HERE

Just before the storm,
flowering trees stand out like fire,
like last year's ghosts, like paint spilled there,

like paint spilled in the air. Water on the plate
beneath the barometer, dripping to the hall floor.

There was a stillness where the chorus of birds
out-voiced the thunder.

ROBOT

The guy down the street built a robot.
On Halloween he would bring it out
to stand there on his porch in the night
in a circle of leaves
and flash and roll and move
its corrugated arms.

I came home from school one day
and the robot was in my bedroom.
In a deal brokered by my father,
the robot had come to live with me.

It was much larger
in my room—it took up a full corner
between the toy box and the closet door—
and while I slept
the optical lens in the centre of its domed head
glowed a non-radiant amber.

Friends came over to see my robot.
I made it roll around on the blood-red
carpet, using the big square control panel
the guy down the street had built for it.
I told my friends about the guy down the street—
his name was Mark, he was a teenager—
and how he built the robot,
played with it for a few years,
and then let my dad bring it home for me.
I made the arms move up and down
with a whine,

and the claw hands
clasped objects proffered
by my friends: ball gloves,
teddy bears, hockey cards, books.

I didn't want the robot
to vanquish my enemies or pester
my sister with its incessant hooting.
I wanted it to impress girls on my behalf.
To help my Dad load the Volvo
early in the morning on the way to the cottage.
To hold one corner
of my fort blankets in its tri-pronged talons
and shine a beam down
to share in the joy of
Daniel Pinkwater and Gordon Korman;
John Bellairs and Paul Zindel—
its righteousness as robust
as its rubber barrel thorax.

And then one day
I wanted to see the full candlepower
of the technology within.
Latches attached the head
to the body. I approached them with
trepidation, expecting to lift
the head and reveal
a density of technology
not meant for human consumption—
an Ark of circuitry
and perpetual motion daemons.

But I found only a few gears, some rusted
metal rods intersecting at various points,
a disappointing mess of wires,
a box down near the bottom
that looked like the undercarriage
of a remote-control car, and a lot of void

filling up an oversized rubber garbage can
with a plastic dome
fitted as a lid, some dryer pipe
rigged up with opposable clamps
for hands, some train-set lights....

A musty smell filled my room.
A week later, my Dad hauled the robot
out to the alley and secreted it away in the Volvo
in the early morning.
I figured he didn't want Mark to catch us
disposing of his creation
and realize he'd been exposed as a fraud
in the field of robotics.

Years later, I found out Mark's father
had given the robot to my dad one morning
while hauling it out to the trash himself.
Mark had gone nuts
and was sent to an asylum.

Years later, I realized he was too old
to be playing with robots
and thought: What a stoner.

VEINS

The ground beneath Centralia, Pennsylvania, has been on fire
for forty-seven years. Explosions where methane pockets
come into contact with the burning vein
rock the houses like earthquakes. There are nine people left.
Smoke vents from the ground.

Closer to home, our son wonders if it would be weird
if everyone on our street had a knife fight.
Just butter knives, he says,
not realizing this is even weirder.

WE LIVE NEAR AL CAPONE

The air mattress heaves as you roll out.
It's too cold for you in this echoing
room in April, half-clothed with ownership;
and you let the dog out to make a first
set of tracks in the near-frosted lawn.
You don't like the paint. You don't like
the jungle-print wallpaper. But you like
the hardwood floors. The floors can stay.
And you come back and sit beside me
in the dull sun.

NOT YET, THOMASIN

I stood in the mellow orange light of a plastic moon
and watched as my son rose in his bed
and reached up, as if grabbing a jar from a high shelf.

Then, with his other arm, he pushed gently in an arc
towards the sheets, before returning his head to the pillow,
never having woken.

In the morning, he does not remember my sitting
on the edge of his bed, pulling the dream-laden shirt
over his sleep-salty head, before folding him
back under the damp sheet, cooled in a July night zephyr—

but he remembers his dream:
his little sister turning into a balloon and floating away,
and how he caught her and brought her back down
to his side.

And he is not devastated by his dream's
power, its ed-film Frenchness, but rather, seems buoyed
by the assurance he's gained in his ability to be
the protector; the boy who anchored his sister to the earth.

But we are stricken
by his success in ballooning, and his proportional failure
in realizing the nightmare. All I can think of for days:
his imprint on the bedclothes, his fever-plastered
brow cooling, his back and flank cooling under my hand

as he slept on, happy but exhausted,
when I thought he was reaching for jars.

FIRE ESCAPE

Drunk after a dance, we climb
to look over the town that whiskey built while it sleeps,
stirring in its autumn nightshirts;

some of us kissing, some of us just breathing stories
above the parking lot where a field once shook
and bent to itself in the dark—

where a redheaded girl sang at lunchtime
and the distillery men dropped grease-spotted paper cones
carrying triangles of sandwich,

hardboiled eggs, and wedges of orange
down the switchback of stairs
for a song from my mother,

who stood in song below the fire escape
in the fresh bread of the wind,

as cookies fell like manna,
and the trains came in.

FORRESTER

What song did your mother sing to you,
she would ask the dying in the hospice,
days or hours before the end.
The meter was not running;
and though her own powers had waned,
no stage could house these tragedies,
no taxi cab could ferry
the hero and the waxing ghost
any better than her voice.

CHRISTMASES

Three men lean on shovels in the snow,
staring at a point in the air.
Carrying twenty-three dollars of kielbasa
wrapped in butcher's paper, on which
I've written an anonymous letter,
I am lured in tighter
by the falconry of their gravitas.
My intent was to finesse this year's
installment between the doors,
a coiled child in swaddling clothes,
but I am insinuated as the fourth—
a father and his grown sons,
a man paying a sausage-based debt—
and introduced to a spot in the chimney
where you can see straight through
to the sky, the pressures of a hundred
Christmases, the attendant winds
and thaws having loosed
the mortar to a space
my son expects fireflies to inhabit
in the summer.

SO LONG, VINCE GUARALDI

Stretched out below Freemasonry, a bear in a track suit,
thrown recklessly around an armchair
against a backdrop of mullions,
cross-hatched against the snowfall,
I'm filling in for the bookstore cat
who punched out at lunch and disappeared
into the alley. I'm under a wooden giraffe,
under the spell of the mystics making hay
in the self-help section, and ready to smash
Vince Guaraldi's piano to fucking pieces
for another note in the alphabetical forest
of this used and rare afternoon, blackballed
like an irreligious libertine
and stripped of acacia laurels.
Just over my shoulder a pictorial biography
of Mother Teresa of Calcutta, 1910-1997.

DISAPPEARER

Take out the creche and argue about
who gets to set up the kings.
—Okkervil River, "Listening to Otis Redding During Christmas"

My God, what we used to do with Jesus,
secreting him away like a delicious white berry,
laying him in the pot-pourri or astride a banana

in the kitchen's hanging basket, blissed-out
in the cold concave manger of the egg tray—
our holidays in the sway of this unorthodox hobby horse.

We committed ourselves to the game in the spirit of the older,
bearded Jesus—the one depicted in *The Golden Treasury*,
surrounded by children, arms outstretched,
in near-hysterics of benevolence and bonhomie.

But this ceramic-and-wood-paste babe of swaddled action
has forsaken the safety of the creche, leaving his parents and the snow-
white lambs to stare into the moulded straw that fits him like a bong case.

Taped to our Lakeland's collar, he luxuriates
in her grizzled coat as he drives her across the Alps
of the boot-printed backyard, like cherubic Hannibal strapped

to his leather howdah, as the magi make their way across the Persia
of the living room, glacial and imprecise.
When he's found and repatriated, it's only to be disappeared by morning,

when he rides the pendulum of the grandfather clock,
weighing off the hours half-naked and serene, and recalibrating
the axis of our home, counter to the shadow of the mullions

slowly morphing across the wall. For one moment every day
they stand cruciform, before another swing marks
enormous movement in the heavens—

a cinematographer's slow scouting around the base
of Golgotha. And over the days of disappearing, the clock
pitches down to a stasis too early, until

winding the heirloom, my father will discover the Christ Child,
clinging to the pendulum,
a stowaway on a stalled amusement-park ride.

He will relocate him to the hand-detailed hay,
bringing the pageant into a new phase as the magi
move in for the old spice-route routine.

And before they can burn a single stick of frankincense,
he is gone again, and nestled like a bug
in the handset

of the old black rotary dial,
which gleams like a muscle of smoke
in the shortbread-scented kitchen.

THE DAY I DIDN'T GO SKYDIVING

We're at the semi-permeable membrane of savagery,
building mansions inside rooms
where the walls become the world all around.

There's a bleeding across barriers by the things
of the forest floor; the ungulates flirting with the ecotone,
their noses capable of following a woman

across several high ranges, through phases of the moon.
And I am moved to a deep harbour with little draft,
where canvases roll like ships through the night,

prison ships without prayer flags,
where we suffer the way people suffer in poems.
So tell me, little night spark,

are you willing to break yourself
against the prow of my window, to trespass
on the unfortunate frictions of estrangement,

taking on the cold warmth of milk,
luxuriating in the matching stars
that bloom like truffles in the blood cinema

of our dark heads as the children hunt
your phantom treasure?
Your ardency would be touching

in someone half your age with twice your talent,
maybe half-American and fully half-in-the-bag.
But tonight's not your night.

I know intimately the experience
of not being burned alive. It's happening to me right now.
I'm just standing here, waiting for the elevator

nonchalantly, preposessedly not burning,
reflecting doors bringing us together at the shoulder,
two sails on an ascending sound.

THURSTON OWL

for Mark G.

You have only one photo of your childhood
and it's of you and a screech owl you captured
and kept as a pet for two years. You had this book
about the animal kingdom and it said screech owls
lived in apple orchards in hollowed-out trees.
It just so happened you hung out in an apple
orchard. So you took a flashlight and went
to the apple orchard at night and reached
into a tree and grabbed a screech owl
and put him in your hat.

You named him Thurston Owl.
All you did was follow the directions.

THE RISE OF THE TORTOISE LOBBY

The first thing that happened when the turtle showed up
on Thanksgiving is we argued about whether
it was a turtle or a tortoise.

Then we argued about whether tortoises,
if it was a tortoise (and we were pretty sure it was
a turtle), are reptiles or amphibians, and then
whether that mattered when it came to it being
cold-blooded, and whether muddied and encrusted
with glittery sand, it could use some water.

So, with a plastic pitcher and an old turkey baster,
the kids and I set to bathing it in tap water
where it lay at the side of my in-laws' house,
a pile of mesclun, arugula, and dandelion greens
under its chin in an effort to give it the strength
to decide whether it was headed to the road or the lake.

The kids took turns squeezing the red baster bulb
and dribbling water until the mud-caked and scrabble-scarred
shell shone like the golden treasure tended with similar husbandry
and scheduled to emerge from the oven a few hours hence.

We'd developed a theory, while sitting around the fire
watching the Lions game, that the tortoise (it's a turtle,
but the tortoise people are putting up a vigorous lobby)
had buried itself in a morass of mud and leaves
at the coming of winter, but had been pulled from its hibernation
by a coyote, a badger, a bobcat, or fox,

and left for a gritty death after losing a back claw
in the battle. But under what must have felt like a deluge
from the turkey basters, our charge rallied, arching up
on its back legs, telescopic claws emerging
from sleeves of sand that wreathed its limbs
like a hideous disease, and within twenty minutes

it had moved with so much ardour towards the lake
I had to lift it, like an elderly relative, over the garden wall.
And while I carried it (its shell as big as the turkey platter),
the claw we initially thought had been chewed off
reached out and gripped my forearm in brotherhood.

When I lay the leviathan down on the lawn approaching the lake,
it opened its heartbreaking, beakless mouth
and an ancient exhalation rocked the beachfront.
We found some tracks in the sand along the break wall later,
and my son claims the turtle startled him on the beach
just before dinner; but I think the tracks were from

its arrival by moonlight, and my son was just trying
to assure me it hadn't gone somewhere to die.

DWELLER ON THE THRESHOLD

Black water pours down where their invisible mouths
pock and register across the surface of the reservoir.

You never fully see one, just a brief ring of bone
eating voraciously in the orchard evening.

There's a little noise associated with all this, like a
a mouth opening to say something...
and folding itself out of sight.

Then it arrives on some unspoken shore,
déjà vu's coelacanth: it walks out of extinction
and empties itself into the vacuous mansion I've built
of the will.

I reach for my boys' hands on the break wall
and steer them back towards the house—
            through late summer flowers bound

for someone's visitation, and fruit trees
            in rings of rotting pear flesh and wasp motion

—to where I'm sweating before a vanity mirror,
            impossibly hungry, and full to the point of illness.

SMALL SHELTER

I'm like the python
who gorges himself into immobility

and becomes a swollen grape leaf
on the forest floor, beneath the canopy
that sustains and tempts and allows.

Before a pretty corpse, a gorgeous meal:
something stuffed with something stuffed:
with wildebeest or gnu, with grasses

and ruminant sugars—
unable to writhe when it's time to writhe,

unable to escape unclockable appetite
and a months-long digestion, an instinct
that pins me down like a worm
on a dissection pan

of jungle loam,
so when the driver ants advance like a strobe
to my shiny, taut side,

and leave my skeleton
to fall into the cruel cage of my last supper—
a pile of bones inside a pile of bones—

something else
will make their nest in us. Maybe
that's why I'm here—

to provide some small creature
some small shelter in the end.

SELF-DIAGNOSIS WITH BULLWHIP

The last shred of muscle in my abdomen died.
Like a slow-drying stain over years it suffered its last
and didn't bother leaving a ghost to ward off
any tissue that might rally itself,
might organize and gather like a storm cloud.

All that remains: a meridional heaviness
with intermittent threats, anecdotes
of what it's like to tear like a beached whale,
some instinct of being rent
like an old, once glorious sheet—

a sheet virgins once lay themselves against.

Now I could not bend to kiss them,
or watch.

NOTHING BY MOUTH AFTER MIDNIGHT

Me and my seasons.
Me and my navel-gazing mornings,
my wrapped-within nights,
the self-decoding afternoons—

honesty returning to the precipice
to perch with perfectly curled feet,
cilices on the bow of my lips, before I look
back into the curving abyss—

these afternoons
when I want so badly to see,
and self pity's diamond-tipped drill

bores into the salt mine of fear.
And I'm just charming enough
to draw you near and drain you
like Lake Peigneur.

So when we're watching TV
and I'm a great lachrymose wreck,
torturing myself with tableaus
of my final moments,

the long-awaited proof
that I actually have a skeleton—
it's rising in me, like veins of salt,
tablets carved with the story of my hunger—

I cry for uncertainty:
a pre-emptive, speculative cry,
because I'm not even sick

in the classical sense.
For now, it's nil by mouth after midnight,
and my organs make ghosts
on a monitor, and they make a little

paper film strip—
a storyboard of blooming rosettes
of cells, or ulcerated tracts of gut;
bags filled with salt-candy deposits,

some horror reaching a tentacle
up from my groin into me
and wrapping around organ and bone
like plantar roots and heart worm.

And when they leave me alone
to wipe the cold medium off my gut,
I try to interpret the images
frozen on the screen.

All I come up with is this.

CYPRUS LAKE

A man who looks like John Ditsky
walks into the shallow, sandy lake.
Rawboned and oiled-up he brings
cold water to his sagging chest
with obvious pleasure. His bathing suit
is baggy and red; his hair is Detroit, 1963.
He showcases his efficient breaststroke;
transitions into a workman-like waltz crawl.
He reminds me of a boxer
in a striped singlet, circling a foe
in the Marquis of Queensbury style.
Nearby, teenaged girls step like does
in the shallows. If I were to come upon
them standing before the mirrors in the wilds
of their own bedrooms, in their bras and panties—
this would contain none of the freedom
and nonchalance of this northern beach,
where I stand paralyzed at the water's edge,
wrestling with the hewn rock
of what I once was, locked in a cask
of what I am. This is not modesty.
This is fear: fear of the modest ripeness
of youth apparent in the half-naked
monolith of now. No one here cares about the past
as much as I do. Not even John Ditsky,
who must be a ghost at Cyprus Lake.

WHITE LIES (ABOUT HACKBERRY EMPERORS)

Using a bucket,
my son has rescued a butterfly
from the shallows of Lake Erie.
It rides the cataract of the rim
as he pours it gently into the grass
above the break wall.
It's a Hackberry Emperor and it walks
the wet lawn
in a mechanical circle, and satisfied
he has saved one of God's
creatures from certain death
in the lake, my son returns
to the beach.

But the Hackberry Emperor
has a ripped wing—
torn and leaking the wet chalk
of its colours. And as I let it crawl
on my hand, to place it away
from further harm,
my daughter approaches
and asks to hold it, too.

It crosses the bridge of our fingers—
from my hand to hers—
her shrieks cast doubt and despair
from the temple of the afternoon
as she is tickled
by its death throes.

We place it on an ornamental
watering can,
and I tell her it will dry in the sun
before flying away.

It will be long gone by the time
they are old enough
to read this.

DEUS EX-MACHINA

In the right-of-way, like ashes, the welders walk in the snow,
reconstituting in the fog or mist
or smoke or gauze.

They're backlit by a many-armed mollusk
that cracks quietly into being, orange and arcing
but felt in the chest through the double glass,

then burning out past black
to grey, then a white that stands out against white,
then veined with a dark contrail and punctuated

with a small falling planet
through the wild carrot and goldenrod, and everything
else pelted with frost and by powder,

the essential blackness glowing underneath.
Some of them bend to their work; others set out
towards the station,

slow enough to accommodate everything so briefly.
And we cannot tell what they're doing there, so suddenly
and slowly,

but they leave two-tone tracks,
their tread pressing down to the soot, like ghosts are milling there,
misting opals around their boot prints, in the gauze,

the smoke, the mist, the fog.
And that's a very quiet second, in which I wonder
whether the train moves, or the city.

SHADOWS OF INDIVIDUAL TRAINS

Let the flight record show, they fucked
in the cabin across the skyline, while the lady on the radio
said the evening was a sweet little *schadenfreude* bomb.
And all the Lego in the landfill was clicking together—
accreting under pressure and becoming the most wonderful thing.
Infinitesimally they hang there, a drink without a glass,
climbing before breaking apart
down the curved outsides of one sphere
into the bathysphere of another.
        There will be individual trains.
There will be the dreams of the shadows of individual trains.
And you're swimming at the metallic beach.
And you're standing at a scale replica of a place
        that doesn't exist, poling through the mist at dawn.
You can plot the great shipwrecks of the Great Lakes
on a bathymetric chart—the apostles, the saints,
and their achievements—
but can you rank the great club foots,
the standard and accepted histories of their deeds
and misanthropies? Can you consult the auspices
in a man's liver, like chicken feed
strewn before the battlefield?

RIVERMOUTH

There's a house at the end of this frozen river,
and a girl who's chagrined that the first man to hit on her
says he can see by the callouses on her fingers
that she plays a guitar, and a blush runs
under the bridge of the white slash
of her scarf, spreading up like blood from the rivermouth,
as he recounts how his binoculars smashed
on the road after an afternoon of watching geese at Stop 26.

He's the kid you met on the beach at the Pinery.
Your family tried to convince him he needed to wear bug spray,
but he said he liked to watch them take flight
from his swollen arms and knuckles,

engorged and irritated like this young lady who burns
like an abandoned house: the abandoned house she grew up in,
burning now.

FULLY ENGULFED

As the house burned on the lake,
boats lit out from it and sailed quietly
to the shore—nothing but a crackle, and no one
remembers them reaching land,
if they did at all.

THEY WILL TAKE MY ISLAND

The gate of your ribs pulled open tonight,
your chest bleeding the ghost of a searchlight.
It picks up the grey gull of a boat against the darkness,
the landing party lit white as embers.

You cannot see the man who lies in the hold
on a dune of dried fruit spilled from crates.
It's as dark as the centre of the sun down there; his thirst
as bright as the centre of that darkness.

Sometimes he looks like that guy you know—
that guy with the boat and the card game.
But most of the time he just looks like the admiral,
locked away in disease from his horde.

It smells like birthday candles where we watch
from the shore. The lamp in your chest has gone out.
The shorebirds hold their eggs inside like the future,
like a new, dark beach before the prow.

TITUS LIVIUS

Before going into battle, Roman generals consulted the auspices.
A representative of the Victim class was eviscerated
where he stood, his steaming auguries spilling
into the dirt. A wise old fellow poked through the pile,
letting the size, shape, condition, and orientation of the liver
determine whether the day would be auspicious
or inauspicious.

This was considered more reliable than the old way—
throwing millet on the ground and divining from the pattern cut
by chickens at feed. Under that antiquated protocol,
too many glorious days turned out super-glorious,
which, though nice for everyone involved, served only
to highlight the overall unreliability of the system,
which led to someone finally finding a use for the Victims,
who had been driving everyone nuts

with their whingeing and need for acceptance.
It was on the way home from a super-glorious sacking—
which the auspices, as foretold by the chicken feed,
said would merely be glorious—
that a general came upon a Victim
enumerating his issues in the streets and,
in a fit of frustration, took his spade and hove the man open
from stem to stern, spilling him where he stood.

The general's seer sidled up, consulted the offal,
and said: *Now,* that *says it's going to be a highly auspicious day.*
Soon, Victims were at a premium, and soon after that,
consulting the auspices was no longer of the *zeitgeist.*
Somewhere in all this sacking, pillaging,
and auspice reading, someone realized that the reason
behind consulting the auspices

was the belief that human action was futile; everything
was predetermined. If you were going into battle,
preparation and strategy were all but useless.
Finding ways to determine whether the fates
were with you or against you was of greater strategic advantage
than having a better army

in numbers, weapons, and tactic.
So how was sacrificing a Victim at the threshold
of battle any different than trying to devise an impenetrable
breast plate or avant-garde flanking manoeuvre?
It wasn't any different. The very act of eviscerating someone,
and consulting the heft and pungency
of their transverse colon,

were just human machinations aimed at out-foxing
determinism, which was like trying to bite your own teeth.
One guy piped up about
how if everything was predetermined then wouldn't
the act of consulting the auspices simply be part of a
predetermined world and therefore shouldn't they just
go on eviscerating and consulting

without fear of hubris or folly?
He was sent off to some Persian outpost.
And so, for a while, Romans marched into the fray
with no thought given to what the auspices might say.

Defeats that would once have been avoided
not through might, but by turning away from the battlefield
if the fates weren't favourable, began to stack up. But so did victories.
In this way, empires came and went.

But no one foresaw the coming logistical nightmare of removing bodies
from the battlefield during the Crusades.
This was solved by carrying a huge cauldron into the Holy Wars,
boiling down the bodies, tipping the fat in a slick over the reeking mud,
and taking only the bones home aboard clattering carts
to feed to the catacombs.

Then, for a long time, nothing of import happened,
though there used to be a hole in Richard II's tomb, allowing devotees
to reach in and touch his head. That is, until someone
stole his jawbone...

Which brings us up to speed, knowing there will come a time
when fireworks night will no longer be an opera
in which veterans of foreign wars stand at the riverfront
and fall to pieces.

THE FOREVER OF OLD ICE

Every ocean has travelled through my face.
The seas that lapped the lips of Pangea
are here in the ductworks that let
from the corners of my eyes, and what were tears
will be oceans again; what were oceans
will be puddles reflecting clouds

and rivers disintegrating.

FROM A HOTEL ALEXANDRA

Living the way we do, kicking
against the seventeen-year cicadas and coloured glass
buried in the hotel stationery,
we've attained the composure of recon units left alone
in the settling fog and the moon—
or is it really a persimmon hanging in the foreground?
I sit in a window of the Alexandra Hotel,
overlooking the snow of a park
and its cake-top footprints,
and I'm picking my coordinates
from a rubric of times
and shades of times; grapes in a gallery bowl
like candy; a winter below the cemetery,
the cross and the mountain.
I'm waiting through this night for a train.
I imagine a wound has been tied off
down on that diamond with a tourniquet of shoelaces;
and jealous secrets about jealousy and secrets
that carry like the weather,
that leave what's in season to change
its sugars and soften for plunder.

METAL GODS IN THE FOOTHILLS

Bombs away on the ghost-white manna fields,
crispy and talking shit in the slow roast
of morning, landing with a horseshoe

flourish, in a yard by a yard by a yard.
Your hemlines are the very replicas
of the glove republics and their first golden stitchings.

The excess hangs loose like labia,
inexplicable and sad, waiting
for the blue sedan and the jocular wide collars

in a small, walled-in garden
where they'll gamble for five hours
in the loose straw and the smell of something.

It becomes us like a hard shell these new bones,
in a year where the bugs make their holes,
and we make metal gods in the foothills.

There will be war: vicious and marrow-soaring.
Someone will tackle a tiger in the forest
and ride it to the final spit

of land. And build a sepulchre there—
all gold and caramel and élan—
and be garrotted, a hero;

laminated in the seed of the clockwinder;
    a plantation for burning
        counted among the most fortuitous of delusions.

    For now the night bends down
to foul you.

THE BAND OF THE CEREMONIAL GUARD

Somewhere in the Gatineau Hills there is a place
for freaks. It's as if a circus train stopped there and unloaded
a menagerie of God's most physically stunning children.

And when the Band of the Ceremonial Guard
came to play, they were forewarned:
this would be their toughest gig.
They were told not to laugh, to not even flinch—

that this was the only place their audience
would ever know peace. It was a refuge for twins
who had enveloped their twin, but maintained a vestige
of a sibling staring out from a window cut into their clothes;

for the plain-looking girls with *vagina dentata*,
chased out of small towns for chewing up the scenery
of its sons and daughters; polio's scuttling scorpions;
ectomorphic giants, striding like hammered gold

through fall's brittle inferno—
the bereft, the tragic, the heartbreaking improbable—
too beautiful to take in or describe; all insulated
by boreal majesty from our monstrous vocabularies.

And when the band unfurled the glorious blast
of their battle hymns, the voice licked everyone clean—
soldier and hidden population—

until no trace of misfortune or pity remained.
The sun kept time on the manicured lawn.
When the final anthem had been played, the players

moved among the inhabitants on the old sanitarium grounds
and were pitied for the sweat that poured
under their scarlets and bearskins.

GREAT WESTERN AMUSEMENTS

Every summer your uncle would walk out of the bush
with his paycheque and a scheme for beating
Crown & Anchor.

Operators would roll the coins that fell from pockets
and collected in a grate beneath the Zipper.
          This was the change you hadn't thrown into the Globe

of Death, to pay for the insurance policy
of the daredevil who rides the interior on a road
          that becomes a salt flat as his wrist flexes into the illusion.

MALT SHAFT

We hadn't the nerve to visit him in the hospital.
We couldn't tell him how he'd leapt in the strobing space
in the guts of the grain elevator,

from one coordinate to the next, a cartoon skeleton
alternating corona and abyss, and the nothingness
before the instant of creation,

gripping the cable with smoke,
and fingers of smoke becoming ash, and how we laughed,
until we cried, passing him rigid as a plank,

up the shaft to daylight,
where our cachinnations rang like demons.

HE DISAVOWS HIS ORIGINAL COYOTE POPULATION ESTIMATE

The county forester rises from his desk,
stands in his office door, listening
to the darkened nature centre,

its glass display cases of taxidermied foxes,
and the muted light of the terrariums
of fox snakes and star-nosed moles.

He calls out a name I can't make out,
then waits for a reply
before returning to his creaky chair

and our phone conversation.
He knows it's too quiet in the woods for a full moon.
He's been asked to make a retraction:

Did I say there *is* ten thousand?
The woodlots would have to be more spacious on the inside
than they are without,

like a house of leaves.
What I meant to say is there *isn't* ten thousand.
We have been shorted ten thousand.

The matter of that many coyotes
has been removed from our woodlots
by a Yaweh-like figure—

as cold and blank as the face of the sea-pocked moon.
And of what remains, I have little to say
to the positive:

They are cunning, elusive.
There could be one under your desk right now.
They can sneak in with your groceries. Watch for their eyes

peering over the jagged edge of the bag.
Listen for them snuffling for crumbs in the carpet
when you leave the room.

There are only two other possibilities, I say:
One, the investigating officer says someone turned up
in the emergency room with a bite wound on his hand—

The naturalist cannot speculate on the affairs
of men, he says. *He can as little divine from their flesh*
as he can direct the moon to wane.

He is not an alienist for the depths of men's hearts.
Off in the distance, a fox snake
unhinges its jaw.

DEBRIS FIELD INVESTIGATION

One night, you receive a telegram on correspondent's stationery
from a ship at anchor in the middle of the Detroit River.

It directs you to a bakery known more for its longevity than its bread
and asks you to arrive alone and unfollowed.

It says nothing of bathymetric charts
or crash-site debris fields, or the investigation of phantom signals—

the standard late-night-telegram stuff.
You set out in the morning rain, arriving at a dirty glass door

at the appointed hour. You've lived here all your life
and never been in this place.

Two men sit in the dark at a table near a window.
They are systematically making their way through a box

of doughnuts. They do not look up when you approach,
your wet shoes echoing

over the creaking hardwood floors.
They're watching something through the rainy window.

One gestures for you to sit in the third chair.
The other gestures for you to help yourself to a bear claw,

which you do, but when you look out the window,
it's not the world out there:

a fortress of Bengal tiger splits a raging torrent
that breaks around the prow of its shoulders,

swirling sea foam around its black and orange flanks,
making tendrils of its great white hull,

drawing a black-lipped smile around its skull.
And this violence is where the street is supposed to be.

Without looking at you, one of the men says:
We need your help with a problem.

It may not sound like much,
but it was pretty good for a Wednesday.

ALSO KNOWN AS THE YO-YO MAN

There used to be whelks and chambered nautiluses
in the sidewalks, a copy of *The Golden Bough*
on every boy's nightstand, and home runs over the twilit
churchyard hedges.

The Senator could still be seen wandering in the rain.
A clown played pitched-down waltzes
from the depths of your sister's toy box,
and mornings began with torch songs belted into a wooden spoon.

Then there was this guy in a mustard-yellow blazer
who would appear on the playground demonstrating Yo-Yos—
only the blazer distinguishing him from the guy who stood
outside the playground with Bible stories fanned out like a card trick.

At some point, someone must have told him
he could no longer push tracts on schoolchildren from a street corner,
and he went home and died of lead poisoning.

During the investigation, everything about the state of the room—
the condition and orientation of what was left in the wing-back;
the radius of the plumage and how it maintained its arc

like a loud peacock's tail to the wainscoting; how this was offset
by the quiet cup of bone left at the top of the blood-starched collar—
all this was balanced against the inferred quality of his suffering.

Did he pare himself down at the first sign of impotence,
sparing his devotees and handlers the spectacle
of his slow unimportance;

or was he an agent greeted in the carpetless echo
by operatives dispatched from their own desperate studios
by a cat's-whisker cadence,

delivered from the linty atmospherics
of what must be the world's worst radio station,
which emanates forever from the receiver

by the drafty windows? Because that's all there was, really.
Just a dry-cleaning bag with a yellow blazer,
a box of little nooses, and a deep frequency pinpointed on a map.

A WIND-AIDED FIRE

Pretend it's eight o'clock again.
No one's dictating anything—
the little cassettes sit stacked in their cases.
Forget about the boxes of bullets
above the bed in the cabin's spare bedroom,

forget about those hunting parties
that used to push off from the mooring mast
in the prototypes for the flaccid dirigible—

those burgeoning balloonists
and their pulleys and ramps and the little men on bikes
who race around the gondola.... And if you can, act
like we're in the cold desert

—among nose cones and tail sections;
pieces for steering, the skeletons of wings.

Re-envision the commodore.
Appreciate his loyalty to hangers-on; the polishing
of the screw until it's the very curve
of resentment.

Luxuriate in how this all started with clowns.
Clowns and seltzer and tears—

              maybe it all started with the tears?
The tears were definitely there first,
like snail silk in the a priori blackness,
spooky and silent as an unplugged theremin.

Sometimes it's just too easy to put it all together
like this. Take note of some things:

the mass exodus of clowns under cover
of a wind-aided fire;
those museums in Mexico
where the cholera mannequins stand around
like ramshackle victims;

the black tape, the black boxes, the spinning,
and the game you want to learn
so you can be found dead playing it;

the black outlines
of antennas backlit by the city;
the low lake levels
and the emerging snarl of shopping carts—

and then the wind.

See them on the move:
            armed with blackjacks and wigs
and false moustaches—
foreign and uncertain and conscious
of their nudity
in the halls of the neighbourhoods.

But patience—
                        patience
and the constancy of storm fronts.

Patience and the palm-bitten nails.
          Patience and the water-borne illness.
                    Patience and the lung-engulfing plague.

We can all laugh.
We can all make casts of each other's
most private places. We can whip ourselves

with the lash of the deafening possible,
and pretend it's still a couple of hours ago.

FROZEN LIKE FLOATING

Twilight's a demented pie crust of plane scars,
holding back the crushed-fruit mess
of the backlighting,

frozen like floating
icicles made visible, the loosestrife
that fires up like hallelujah,

hanging invisible zeppelins.
How easily this all could've been
something else.

NOTES & ACKNOWLEDGEMENTS

"We Press to Each Other Through the Glass of Days" is after "Four Red Zodiacs" by Lucia Perillo.

"Barn Burning" stems from an infatuation with the chair Abraham Lincoln was sitting in when he was assassinated while watching Tom Taylor's play *Our American Cousin* at Ford's Theatre in Washington, D.C., on April 14, 1865. The chair is on permanent display at the Henry Ford Museum in Dearborn, Michigan.

Love Bombing After the Earthquake by Demetri Vacratsis and *The Holding Room* by John-Anthony Nabben are the stage plays referred to in "Who Has Seen the Muslin Bear?"

"The Beautiful Lake" mentions several paintings by Montreal painter Janet Werner, most specifically "Survivor."

"Small Shelter" is after Thomas Lux's poem "Driver Ant."

"Rivermouth" is for Johnny West.

"Titus Livius" was inspired by Michael Moran, who told me some hilarious Livy anecdotes while browsing in Juniper Books one afternoon. Other Michael Moran anecdotes resulted in "The Band of the Ceremonial Guard," "Great Western Amusements," and "Malt Shaft."

"From a Hotel Alexandra" is after "Harvest" by Louise Glück, and was written in Room 501 of the Alexandra Hotel in Toronto on March 1, 2010.

"Metal Gods in the Foothills" is after "El Oro de los Tigres" by Jorge Luis Borges.

"He Disavows His Original Coyote Population Estimate" is for Bill Harris, who also inspired the opening lines of "New Orchid Society," for which Sephora Pojola provided the closing image.

"A Wind-Aided Fire" is after "The Stagnation" by James Galvin.

References are made throughout to shortwave number stations and the Conet Project recordings (Irdial Discs). Tune in.

Earlier versions of some of these poems appeared in *OffSIDE, Forget Magazine,* the anthology *Tough Times: When the Money Doesn't Love Us* (Black Moss Press, ed. John B. Lee), and Paul Vermeersch's They Will Take My Island online poetry project. Thank you to the editors of these publications.

Several people have provided encouragement, inspiration, support, places to sleep, places to write, and, most importantly, friendship during the writing of these poems: Paul Vermeersch, Sean Grayson, Michael Haggert, Brett Eugene Ralph, Marty Gervais, Lenore Langs, Mary Ellen Scully Mosna, Stephen Pender, Nyla Matuk, Dawn Kresan, Salvatore Ala, Marko Sijan, Jeff Latosik, Jacob McArthur Mooney, Mary Ann Mulhern, Vanessa Shields, Dan Wells, Alexander MacLeod, Mike and Len Epp, Melanie Janisse, Karen Schindler and the good people of Poetry London, Roger Wurdemann and Carl Harris at Juniper Books, the good people at Taloola Café, my students in the Creative Writing Workshops at Mackenzie Hall, and my fellow Waker Glass bandmates, Jake Dimmick, Mark Gelinas, Terry Lusk, and John Pilat.

A special thank-you and acknowledgement goes to the Windsor Endowment for the Arts and their Emerging Artist in Literary Arts Grant.

This collection would not be possible without the ongoing support and encouragement of my editor Stuart Ross and Mansfield Press publisher Denis De Klerck. They knew there was a book here, seemingly before I did. Thank you, Stuart and Denis.

My wife, Jennifer, our three children, my family, friends—they are all part of the transmitter. I am but the receiver.

Robert Earl Stewart's first collection of poetry, *Something Burned Along the Southern Border* (Mansfield Press, 2009), was shortlisted for the Gerald Lampert Memorial Award. His poems have been published in journals in Canada, the U.S., and Great Britain. In 2010, he received the Windsor Endowment for the Arts' grant for Emerging Artist in Literary Arts. He is the lead singer of the band Waker Glass, and lives in Windsor with his wife and their three children. He is working on a novel.

OTHER BOOKS FROM MANSFIELD PRESS

POETRY

Stephen Brockwell & Stuart Ross, eds., *Rogue Stimulus: The Stephen Harper Holiday Anthology for a Prorogued Parliament*
Diana Fitzgerald Bryden, *Learning Russian*
Alice Burdick, *Flutter*
Gary Michael Dault, *The Milk of Birds*
Pier Giorgio Di Cicco, *Early Works*
Christopher Doda, *Aesthetics Lesson*
Rishma Dunlop, *Metropolis*
Jason Heroux, *Emergency Hallelujah*
Jeanette Lynes, *The Aging Cheerleader's Alphabet*
David W. McFadden, *Be Calm, Honey*
Leigh Nash, *Stray Dog Embassy*
Lillian Necakov, *The Bone Broker*
Peter Norman, *At the Gates of the Theme Park*
Natasha Nuhanovic, *Stray Dog Embassy*
Catherine Owen & Joe Rosenblatt, with Karen Moe, *Dog*
Corrado Paina, *Souls in Plain Clothes*
Jim Smith, *Back Off, Assassin! New & Selected Poems*
Robert Earl Stewart, *Something Burned Along the Southern Border*
Priscila Uppal, *Winter Sport: Poems*
Steve Venright, *Floors of Enduring Beauty*
Brian Wickers, *Stations of the Lost*

FICTION

Marianne Apostolides, *The Lucky Child*
Kent Nussey, *A Love Supreme*
Marko Sijan, *Mongrel*
Tom Walmsley, *Dog Eat Rat*

NON-FICTION

Pier Giorgio Di Cicco, *Municipal Mind*
Amy Lavender Harris, *Imagining Toronto*